IMAGES
of England

BEDFORDSHIRE
1940s-1990s

NORTHAMPTONSHIRE

CAMBRIDGESHIRE

Great Ouse

Shelton

Dean

Pertenhall

Melchbourne

Wymington

Riseley

Keysoe

Souldrop

BEDFORDSHIRE

Sharnbrook

Thurleigh

Bolnhurst

Odell

Pelmersham

Bletsoe

Colmworth

Harrold

Chellington

Milton
Ernest

Wilden

Pavenham

Ravensden

Roxton

Great Ouse

Stevington

Oakley

Renhold

Tempsford

Great
Barford

Blunham

Everton

Great Ouse

Bromham

BEDFORD

Potton

Cockayne Hat

Biddenham

Willington

SANDY

Sutton

Wrestlingwor

Moggerhanger

Harrowden

Cardington

Northill

Elstow

Ickwell

Wootton

Old
Warden

Stewartby

Haynes

Southill

BUCKINGHAMSHIRE

Cranfield

Marston
Moretaine

Henlow

Astwick

Salford

Lidlington

Clophill

Millbrook

Maulden

Meppershall

AMPTHILL

Plitton

Aspley Guise

Ridgmont

Steppingley

Silsoe

Shillington

Husborne Crawley

Woburn

Eversholt

Westoning

Pulloxhill

Barton

Shillington

Milton
Bryan

Pegsdon

HERTFORDSHI

Heath
& Reach

Battlesden

Toddington

Sharpenhoe

Hockliffe

Tebworth

Sundon

Miles

LEIGHTON
LINSLADE

Eggington

LUTON

Kilometres

Stanbridge

Totternhoe

Eaton Bray

DUNSTABLE

Caddington

Hyde

Kensworth

Whipsnade

Studham

HERTFORDSHIRE

IMAGES
of England

BEDFORDSHIRE
1940s-1990s

Eric Meadows

TEMPUS

Barton, 8 March 1947. The winter of 1946-47 was exceptionally long and hard in Britain; food, clothing and fuel were all rationed. Snow lay for weeks, with continuous frost but also some sunshine, as here, north of Leet Wood.

First published 2002

Tempus Publishing Limited
The Mill, Brimscombe Port,
Stroud, Gloucestershire, GL5 2QG

British Library Cataloguing in Publication Data.
A catalogue record for this book is available from the British Library.

ISBN 0 7524 2654 0

Typesetting and origination by Tempus Publishing Limited
Printed in Great Britain by Midway Colour Print, Wiltshire

Contents

Moggerhanger Park, with its Soane mansion, is on a low, wooded ridge of the greensand south of the Ouse valley and faces east across the Ivel vale. The park was landscaped by Humphry Repton in 1792, when he planted isolated trees: cedars, walnuts, a London plane, many oaks and hollies and a champion copper beech – two grafts on the same common beech. Shown here is the trunk of the largest copper beech in Britain. 4 December 1998.

Introduction

This book considers the historic county of Bedfordshire – the smallest in area of the English shires – together with Luton, to show the changes that have taken place over half a century. To those who do not know the district, it may seem an unremarkable part of southeast England. It has a wholly man-made landscape that combines the various characteristics of its immediate neighbouring counties, but it is an area of great variety and contrast. The downs give the widest views, but the land is too flat to see a great distance. The central ridge of greensand also offers good views to the north, the south, and across the Ivel vale, and there are most pleasing outlooks along and across the winding valley of the Great Ouse. Perhaps more rewarding is the closer scene, of the little coombes and hollows among the hills. The landscape here is an intimate one with attractive nooks almost everywhere. As well as variations of weather and light, there are the changes of season – the tracery of trees in winter, then the bright greens of spring, followed by blossom early in summer and then gold and russet as the leaves fall.

In common with the rest of southern England, the changes in the county have been dramatic and fairly rapid. The population has doubled; the majority of people live in the Luton-Dunstable conurbation, Bedford-Kempston and about five small towns; the workplace for almost all the people is in these urban centres, as villages are mainly inhabited by commuters; farming now employs very few people, perhaps one-sixth of the number working on the land fifty years ago.

The undeveloped space in many villages has been infilled with new houses and the original cottages and houses have been altered, often by former urban dwellers that have held on to their urban attitudes. As a result, the villages have lost much of their individuality and charm; in fact, some have become islands of suburbia. Built-up areas together occupy about 15% of the land.

It may be a surprise that almost 75% of land in the county is farmed, mainly arable ground of which half is used for growing wheat and barley. Most of the land is intensively-managed monoculture, where anything other than the crop is a weed or pest to be treated accordingly. Bedfordshire has always been an agricultural area. In the nineteenth century its rich cornland on the heavy clay-with-flints yielded straw for straw plait and the hat industry, while lighter soils on sand and gravel gave early vegetable crops from market gardens. In the 1930s there was mixed farming for milk and meat, and vegetables grown both for sale and for stock feed. A lot of ground was sown with cereals, as the soil and climate suited them, but much land was also left as rough pasture. These poor pastures were ploughed in wartime, when ley and crops were alternated and sugar beet was cultivated. In 1947 the government began to subsidize food production. This gave farmers the finance to mechanize – with tractors, spreaders, sprayers, combined drills and combine harvesters – which increased production but made many workers redundant. To accommodate the machines, fields were enlarged by removal of trees and hedges. Farms became fewer and larger. All but the steepest hill slopes could be, and were, ploughed.

Marshes, especially water meadows, have been drained, the rivers dredged and straightened for quicker flow and the meadows changed to arable fields or ley. Instead of hay, silage is made from sown ryegrass. Chemical fertilizers, weedkillers, pesticides and fungicides have been readily used. From 1972 the Common Agricultural Policy has accelerated these changes, encouraging larger, more powerful and sophisticated machines and greater intensity of production. More farmers own their farms. Recently, market gardening has declined.

About 68% of land in the county is intensively farmed, and there the loss of wild flowering plants is almost total, though poppies sometimes bloom for one season. Many marsh species have been lost through drainage and are missing from riverbanks due to realignment. Before the Second World War the hayfields, water meadows and downland pastures had a dazzling display of flowers in spring and summer, the thick vegetation swarming with insects of all kinds, crawling, leaping and flying, such as clouds of flitting butterflies, six-spot burnet moths resting on long grass stems, and chirring grasshoppers. On summer days in the country there was always a cloud of flies buzzing round one's head. Now insects have been more than decimated. Most songbirds are insect or seed-eaters; hence the catastrophic decline in numbers of birds of most species. The loss seems to have been in the last twenty-five years. Swallows and house martins

Luton, 20 August 1964. A red-painted Massey Ferguson combine harvester on Manor Farm, Stopsley, driven by the farmer, Pat Shaw. The man on the tractor is C.W. ('Jack') Chandler who worked and lived on the farm for over thirty years.

no longer fill the summer sky or congregate very noticeably in September for migration. Flocks of lapwings in winter are a rare sight. Even starlings are much less abundant. Skylarks, often several at a time, used to trill in the sky, but now most people may hear only a single bird occasionally. Two centuries ago Dunstable inns served larks as a delicacy to coach travellers, with up to three hundred larks netted on the downs in one night. Cheeping groups of house sparrows were commonplace, but this familiar bird does not breed now in many places. Even the song thrush is often not a regular suburban resident. Looked at superficially, much of the countryside may appear similar now to the way it did in mid-century, but in reality retains only a shadow of its former richness. Under political and agribusiness pressure, driven by the European Economic Community and now the European Union, the agriculture industry has ravaged and severely impoverished the countryside.

Hedges in many parts of the county contain suckering English elm, *Ulmus procera*, planted originally by man and encouraged to spread sideways. If neglected the bushes grow into tall trees. Towering elms with billowing heads of foliage used to line our hedgerows, often a row looking alike, having been grown from the same clone. They were the commonest of trees when, in the 1970s, a flare-up of Dutch elm disease killed almost all the mighty trees. A few specimens of the East Anglian elm, *Ulmus minor*, have survived in the north-east of the county, but they do not produce the rich golden foliage in the autumn. Young English elms have grown from the suckers to about 20ft, but then they usually succumb to the disease. Majestic elms will grace our landscape again but it may not be for another century.

Chellington, 30 October 1980. In contrast to the extensive arable farmland is this old pasture with remains of ridge and furrow on a hilltop above the Great Ouse. The redundant church (diocesan youth centre) stands alone, as the village moved down to the road approaching Harrold bridge. The graceful broach spire is fourteenth century. The early sixteenth-century spire of Harrold soars above trees in the valley (see page 112).

The remaining 9-10% of the county, that which is not built-up or farmed, has diverse uses. As people have more leisure and are able to travel, much land is used for their recreation. Woods, plantations, copses and scrub grow on about $4\frac{1}{2}$% of the land (the average for England is 8%). The trees are about half broadleaf and half conifers, as plantations or planted in broadleaf woods. The Woodland Trust owns three primary woods: Bramingham Wood, Luton, which is community-managed with some coppicing; Kempston Wood and Holcot Wood, which is part of newly-planted Reynold Wood, a hundred hectares on the slopes and skyline at the south end of devastated Marston vale. Eight more woods have public access, perhaps the best being Maulden Wood, Potton Woods and the coppiced lower part of Marston Thrift. Flooded clay pits have made new lakes – one at Stewartby has been taken over for watersports and by waterfowl, especially in winter; other lakes in Ouse valley gravel pits are now nature reserves or in country parks. Sheep and rabbits grazing on the downs for centuries caused flower-filled turf with fine grasses, but sheep farming became uneconomic about 1930. Since then much hawthorn scrub has developed, suppressing the grassland flora especially on the scarp, and despite the efforts of various owners to control it by periodic grazing or occasional clearance by conservation volunteers, it tends to increase. For people to roam and appreciate the views and wildlife, there are three stretches of downs above Luton and two at Dunstable, with Totternhoe Knolls to the west; also four tracts rise between Sundon and Pegsdon, of which two are nature reserves. Wallabies have kept the sward short on Whipsnade Downs! Heath on the greensand is now minimal as pinewoods have been planted by the Woburn and Southill estates on such land, but a little survives in Stockgrove Country Park at Heath and Reach, at Cooper's Hill and in the park at Ampthill. Landscape gardens to enjoy are Wrest Park gardens, Silsoe, and the Swiss gardens at Old Warden. Of local parks the ultimate one must be the deer park of Woburn Abbey, extending over 1% of the county and including the largest safari park in Britain.

Acknowledgements

I gratefully acknowledge the help of the following: Eric Brandreth (former Harpenden librarian), David Henden, Maureen Brown of Leighton Linslade Local History Research Group, Dorothy Richards of Moggerhanger House Preservation Trust, the staff of Bedfordshire and Luton Records & Archives Service, and Bedfordshire County Council Department of Environment and Economic Development for their publication *Bedfordshire in Figures*, Spring 1998.

One
Downland

Caddington, 25 May 1952. In Aley Green, Piper's Farm had a fifteenth-century 'Wealden' house facing south-west to the yard, with barns on three sides. It showed wattle and daub as well as later local brick infill. It was demolished in 1956.

Caddington, 25 August 1960. At Woodside, this mid-nineteenth-century row of cottages for farm workers is built of flint, with brick for arches, quoins and chimneys.

Caddington, 23 August 1959. The green, with its ancient lime trees, of this former farming village seen from the churchyard gates on a summer morning.

Hyde, 26 June 1965. From 1764 'Capability' Brown laid out the 1,500-acre park of Luton Hoo, with a double lake, and planted cedars, oaks, limes and sweet chestnuts to create a magnificent setting for the mansion. This sailing regatta was for RNLI funds.

Hyde, 2 July 1968. The parterre with roses and a domed stone summerhouse by Mewès, viewed from an upper south window of Luton Hoo mansion. In 1999 Luton Hoo was sold.

Luton, 22 August 1948. Bailey Hill water tower, built 1901 in Arts and Crafts style, when it was topped by a tall wind vane, seen from Memorial Park.

Luton, 14 July 1968. Small hat factories on the south-east side of Cheapside. The one on the left was built in 1881 as a house and straw-hat manufactory combined. Originally all the sewing was done by hand. (For its history see *Bedfordshire Magazine* Vol. 26 pp278-80.)

Luton, 23 May 1962. From People's Park above Bell's Close, the south end of the town can be seen lying in the valley. The medieval parish church is between the electricity station and the 1956-57 technical college, backed by the trees of Luton Hoo and Bailey Hill tower.

Luton, 16 July 1968. From People's Park above Bell's Close, central Luton before the Arndale Centre and many tower blocks had been built. The chimneys are at the works built around 1902 for Barford Brothers, bleachers and dyers, and later used by Corona soft drinks.

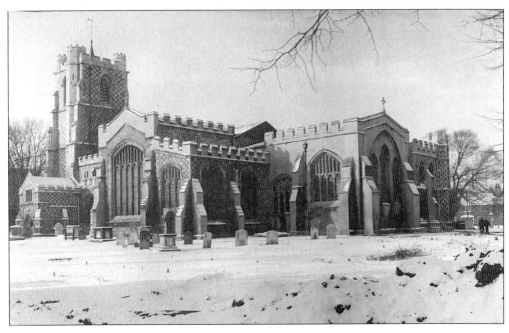

Luton, 10 December 1967. Parish church of St Mary from the south-east when pegs marked the foundation lines for the hall and offices extension. Houses in Church Street face the churchyard elm.

Luton, 8 March 1958. From Wardown Park to the railway bridge, New Bedford Road, seen here from Studley Road, is bordered by the river Lea and horse chestnut trees. The tree-lined road was the Sunday afternoon parade for the populace from 1920-60.

Luton, 25 July 1967. Stuart Street linked Chapel Street to Dunstable Road. On the left is the former magistrates' court and police station (now demolished), designed by Sir Albert Richardson and built in 1936. The prominent spire is at King Street Congregational church, built in 1865 and demolished in 1970.

Luton, 6 June 1968. Stuart Street as it was during construction of the inner ring road looking south-east to the viaduct over Chapel Street.

Luton, 12 October 1963. The older part of the town seen from the west on the downs, at Wellhouse Close on Farley Hill estate. Landmarks include the gasworks, Hart Lane water tower, the town hall tower and, beyond it, airport hangars.

Luton, 9 July 1964. Countryside in the borough: brick and flint cottages built in the 1850s and a weatherboarded barn at Common Farm on Stopsley Common. All were demolished in 1981 after vandalism. Pat Shaw of Manor Farm is on his tractor.

Dunstable, 7 May 1960. The imposing town hall in High Street North seen on a Saturday morning – market day. It was an ornate building of yellow brick and stone, with bas-reliefs, built in 1880 using the pillars of the late Georgian town hall burnt in 1879. The town hall pictured here was demolished in July 1966, its place being taken by a plain red-brick block of offices.

Kensworth, 23 December 1985. The huge quarry from which chalk is pumped as slurry in a pipeline to the cement works at Rugby. To the east, beyond the mast, are Luton airport and Vauxhall works six miles away. This view from Common Road is now obscured by trees.

Dunstable, 30 May 1955. Part of the Marshe Almshouses or Ladies Lodge in Church Street endowed by Blandina Marshe and built in 1743 for six poor maiden gentlewomen. The front was originally stone. Cow parsley can be seen flowering on the verge.

Studham, 18 April 1974. In the south of the county, churches are built of flint and dressed Totternhoe stone (clunch) dug from the lower chalk at Totternhoe. This font of Totternhoe stone has a late Norman round bowl carved with a band of foliage-eating dragons, but early stiff-leaf ornament on the base, which is an upturned font bowl. The carving was done in around 1218 for the church's consecration in 1220, probably by an old and a young mason working together.

Studham, 3 March 1961. Hill Farm with a giant English elm and shadows of more elms across the pasture.

Whipsnade, 13 March 1982. The medieval church was given a brick tower in the sixteenth century, then there was a Georgian rebuild of the nave – locally-made red and vitreous brick chequer, with stone for window and door surrounds. The use of brick makes it an unusual old church.

Totternhoe , 20 July 1957. Totternhoe Knolls viewed from the west on the road to Eaton Bray. The little hill had a Saxon lookout house, and is the site of what was once the county's strongest Norman castle. A lot of grass shows on the slopes of the north-west bailey and higher motte, seen above a prune orchard (which is still there today). The large tree is an elm.

Whipsnade, 18 June 1960. A pool for flamingoes, geese and ducks in front of the restaurant in the former farmhouse. The Zoological Society of London opened the zoo (now Wild Animal Park) on the downs here in 1931.

Totternhoe, 14 September 1998. Totternhoe has a lovely church that was mostly rebuilt in the late fifteenth century of local stone dug from under the north side of the Knolls, a hill on the lower chalk. The building has fine battlements, pinnacles and flushwork, all displays of wealth. Totternhoe stone weathers badly, so this view is soon after the latest maintenance of the exterior.

Totternhoe, 24 August 1974. The rebuilding was done for a prosperous villager named Ashwell, as recorded by this rebus on the north arcade.

Eaton Bray, 8 September 1956. Open country to the downs of Dunstable and Eaton Bray when there was only a little hawthorn scrub on the slopes, seen from a lane south-east of Bellows Mill. A light biplane is towing a glider. These must have been some of the last shocks of corn to be seen in the county. Distant Icknield Farm (centre-right) now has many more buildings but no trees to hide them.

Eaton Bray, 7 August 1987. Originally there was common grazing on the downs of Eaton Bray. This drover's road, up to 15ft lower than the bank, was worn into the scarp by the feet of animals and men over many centuries, and may be one track of the ancient Icknield Way.

Sundon, 30 July 1961. Rough grass and flowers on chalky ground just west of the hill road down to Harlington, looking north-east over elms in hedgerows on the gault vale to Sharpenhoe Clapper, the distinctive and well-known landmark owned by the National Trust. The viewpoint is now in woodland.

Sundon, 3 August 1987. From Sundon Hills Country Park (Bedfordshire County Council) looking north over fields on the gault plain to Harlington, with the wooded greensand ridge on the skyline. The park has open grazing and an old chalk quarry, both with typical chalk flowers, and also patches of scrub woodland.

Sharpenhoe, 12 August 1956. Sharpenhoe Clapper seen from the north with a lot of grass on the slopes now covered by a thicket of bushes. Clouds are gathering from the south-west.

Sharpenhoe, 25 April 1954. The small hamlet among elms seen from the north end of Sharpenhoe Clapper, with a central farm beyond the left birch. This farm has been replaced by black and white dwellings which, with other houses, make a larger and unattractive hamlet divorced from the land.

Sharpenhoe, 26 August 1956. The path along the top edge of the scarp, just west of Sharpenhoe Clapper's beech grove and near the south corner, gave the view to the south over flowery sward. Now a barbed-wire fence (which periodically confines grazing sheep) follows the path's lower edge, and a large beech hides most of the slope; also little grass is visible on the far hilltop where the road up Moleskin is in a cutting.

Sharpenhoe, 22 January 1967. A group of haystacks at Grange Farm; one is thatched, as the farmer liked to maintain his skills by continuing some of the traditional practices.

Sharpenhoe, 22 January 1967. C. Rook, the farmer of Grange Farm, with a pet ewe and lambs. The farm buildings were all demolished in July 1995.

Sharpenhoe, 2 July 1983 (above) and 18 August 1989 (below). The view to Barton from the east slopes of The Clappers before and during the construction of the Barton bypass. The banks became less obvious when covered with grass. The additional road with traffic is another change to this landscape. Chalk for the embankments came from under the hilltop field to the east of Barton cutting.

Barton, 8 March 1947. Snow in the valley among the rounded Barton Hills showing, towards the right, above the springs, a drover's track up the slope which is nowadays hidden in a wood. The snow was almost untrampled because the village was a small one; also there were hardly any cars and their use was limited, so few people were out.

Barton, 8 March 1947. Elms on the west side of the valley below Leet Wood.

Barton, 25 April 1948. The same large elm in young leaf, but looking north-east.

32

Barton, 27 July 1946. View from Barton Hills above the springs, looking down to the elms that hid the west side of the small village. The grassy area among the bushes on the left slopes has now become woodland.

Barton, 25 February 1956. From the south edge of Leet Wood, this was the view eastwards to the head of the folded coombe. The stream from the springs flows under the central line of trees and bushes.

Barton, 8 August 1957. The springs valley or coombe was carved out of the chalk by ice sheets and the meltwater from them. The east side of the coombe has a cluster of lovely rounded ridges and humps with hollows between them. The villagers named them Plum-Pudden, Flagstaff, The Steps, Stairway and Bonfire Knoll. Here is a view to the north from above the springs on a sunny evening. At that time there had been no grazing, so the grasses were tall, with thistles among them, but no sign of the hawthorn scrub that was to come; rabbits had kept it in check until the

mid-1950s. Later the hills had a surrounding fence and were grazed with cattle, but scrub still increased, so some of it was cleared and sheep reintroduced. In 1982 the Barton Hills were designated a National Nature Reserve for their chalk flora. Most splendid is the Pasqueflower on the steepest slopes, but there are orchids, trefoils, thyme, rockrose and Chiltern gentian, among other plants, and cowslips are increasing. Rabbits are back and expose chalk on some slopes. Exmoor ponies now graze the nature reserve in winter.

Barton, 6 November 1949. From the east top of the Barton Hills looking to Sharpenhoe Clappers beyond Leet Wood. The grassed steep on the left of the wood is now lost in scrub.

Barton, 12 August 1956. A seventeenth or eighteenth-century timber-framed house divided into three cottages, Nos 71-73 High Street.

Barton, 15 November 1964. Riders emerging from Leet Wood, a beech grove on the west crest of the coombe, with other trees on the lower slope. Below is the west edge of the village and Pulloxhill in the distance.

Barton, 6 April 1957. The water mill in derelict state. It was probably built in 1852, and was restored in 1974.

Pulloxhill, 24 August 1963. The prospect to Barton Hills reveals the many elms on the gault plain, almost hiding Barton in the centre. The less steep slopes of the eastern hills have been made into cornfields. The original Hillfoot Farm is in the foreground.

Pulloxhill, 11 March 1961. The road uphill to the village passes the seventeenth-century former Hillfoot Farm, with entry to the present farm on the right. The shadow of an elm is cast across the road.

Pegsdon, 10 August 1952. From the Barton to Hitchin Road, cornfields occupied the lower slopes of the downs, but their steeper sides and coombes were used for grazing. Lynchets near Deacon Hill can be seen on the left and the 'peak' is towards the right.

Pegsdon, 4 October 1964. Cattle grazing stubble, looking east to Deacon Hill from the north-west corner of the land now owned by the local Wildlife Trust, who have returned the fields to flowery grassland.

Pegsdon, 23 June 1966. The name Pegsdon means 'valley by a peak' and this is it. The view is south-east up the great coombe and shows the small amount of scrub. This is part of the Wildlife Trust nature reserve.

Pegsdon, 9 June 1968. Looking north-west down the great coombe with limited scrub on the west side, where it is now dense except for cleared viewpoints. The two fields are becoming flowery meadows, except for a fenced plot, which is harrowed for weeds of arable.

Two
Gault and Greensand

Shillington, 21 April 1961. The church is on top of a low chalk hill with views all round, over open country to the west. Here the churchyard was full of flowering cow-parsley above Church Street and the gault vale to the east.

Shillington, 7 May 1961. On the road to Henlow, a former country pub, The Marquis of Granby, and an orchard. It is now a private house.

Shillington, 15 February 1958. The sixteenth-century Old Court House in Apsley End, when it was visible from the road. Nowadays it is behind a high conifer hedge.

Shillington, 25 January 1978. In marshy Church Panel at Woodmer End is an earthwork, a Danish fortified camp from the late ninth century. It is a broad mound on the south-west bank of a once-navigable stream, with an outer bank and ditch on the other sides. Here is part of it in a grazed pasture, looking towards the redundant Lower Gravenhurst church.

Silsoe, 19 July 1958. A pony and trap in the lane coming from Maulden, when this was a most unusual sight.

Silsoe, 11 July 1981. At Wrest Park are wide formal gardens made 1706-1740 and later modified and restored. On the site of the earlier house, this marble fountain and statuary face the far Pavilion beyond the Long Water.

Silsoe, 19 June 1960. In Wrest gardens, the banqueting Pavilion of 1709-11, a rare piece of English baroque designed by Thomas Archer. The statue, by Carpentière, is of William III.

Silsoe, 15 September 1946. High Street, the A6 Luton-Bedford road on a summer morning when motor traffic was very limited. The gabled house included the village shop and post office.

Clophill, 10 January 1959. At Cainhoe, a cast-iron griffin on a gate pier by a continuation of the drive from the north-east lodges of Wrest Park. This drive used to lead to the nearest railway station at Shefford.

Westoning, 26 March 1986. The house of Westoning Manor (private apartments) is an attractive building, Jacobean in style, built of red brick and stone in 1843. The south and east fronts can be seen here.

Flitton, 19 June 1960. In High Street, a little east of the church, three cottages in a row have different roof coverings, thatch, tiles and slates. They are now partly hidden by shrubs.

Toddington, 12 January 1958. The fine cruciform church, its exterior dating from the early sixteenth century, which crowns the hilltop. Around the large irregular green are good houses, mostly of local brick. The cast-iron pump is late Georgian.

Toddington, 21 May 1956. Mill Farm, by Fancott bridleway, has the abandoned water mill next to farmer Wild's house facing the yard. Elms form the background to these interestingly varied buildings.

Toddington, 3 February 1957. Ramblers on a rutted farm road to Herne Green Farm, west of Toddington, passing a stackyard.

Toddington, 30 September 1956. Feoffee Farm at Fancott has a small timber-framed house, seen here from a pasture, showing how typical grassland used to look.

Tebworth, 20 March 1960. At Buttercup Farm the eighteenth-century house, of chequered red and vitreous local brick, faces the yard where hens peck and scratch. Elms line the hedge behind it.

Tebworth, 16 February 1995. The same property, considerably enlarged, is now the home of an affluent businessman.

Hockliffe, 7 May 1960. Leafy and rural Church End is on the low hill to the west. A seventeenth-century timber-framed farmhouse is seen here from the churchyard, backed by elms. Buildings by Watling Street in the valley are almost hidden by elms.

Hockliffe, 27 July 1963. The village developed naturally along the main road, Watling Street (A5), to benefit from passing trade. The houses were mostly built of brick in the latest fashion. This refined early Georgian row of local brick is next to the Woburn road and faces the Leighton-Linslade turning.

Battlesden, 23 April 1981. A rural backwater in farmed countryside, this view from the lane looks south towards the few houses of the village in the valley and over the hollow to trees near Hockliffe church on the farther hilltop. The Chiltern hills can be seen above Tring on the horizon.

Stanbridge, 21 February 1960. At the east end of the village is this seventeenth-century house, until recently divided into a pair of cottages, in an orchard.

Leighton Buzzard, 8 September 1957. A house in North Street, latterly called Holly Lodge, which was still impressive in its dereliction. It was a late Tudor timber-framed house with cross-wings, all faced with brick in 1690 as recorded on the weathered stone, 'T B y1690'. Thomas Baskerfield, a young and wealthy maltster who married Mary Fuller in 1691, bought it in 1689 from the maltster family of Poole. At the time it must have been the most handsome house in the town. It was lived in until 1936, later became the Co-op potato store, and was demolished in 1967-68 to widen West Street as the main route for through traffic.

Opposite: Linslade, 27 January 1957. On the towpath of the Grand Union Canal, with oaks, willows and a glimpse of the Manor Farmhouse of Old Linslade.

Linslade, 21 February 1960. The little river Ouzel cuts through the greensand ridge on the south-west boundary of the county. This is the prospect north across the Ouzel valley, from above the railway tunnel and over the bridge on the Bletchley road. Here is Old Linslade, where the medieval church and early eighteenth-century Manor Farmhouse of red and vitreous brick are almost encircled by the canal.

Eggington, 9 October 1955. The south front of the house of Street Farm, which shows its sixteenth-century timber frame with an overhanging cross-wing, and also a nineteenth-century extension of yellow brick, and altered windows.

Eggington, 6 September 1974. More recently it has had further additions and alterations.

54

Heath and Reach, 20 May 1962. At Fox Corner is this picturesque house of a smallholding, where a pig can be seen in the orchard.

Milton Bryan, 18 April 1964. At midday in spring, a farm worker has parked his tractor outside the Red Lion with its diapered brickwork and ornate bargeboards. There is Victorian iron fencing by the path.

Woburn, 30 April 1967. The central town hall, designed by Edward Blore, was built in 1830.

Woburn, 20 September 1953. At the central crossing in the beautiful Georgian village, looking to the whitened front of the Bedford Arms Hotel in George Street and facing the green.

Woburn, 30 April 1967. Facing High Street, the front of the old parsonage when in disrepair. It has since been restored as a house and antiques shop. It is a stately building designed by Sir William Chambers and built in 1756. Beyond it, on the old church site, is the 1865 mortuary chapel (Woburn Heritage Centre) and the sandstone tower rebuilt by Blore in 1830, who capped it with the charming adornment.

Woburn, 21 March 1995. Fronting the old churchyard, the school that was built in 1582 and restored by Blore. It is still a school today.

Woburn Abbey, 23 March 1958. Mighty oaks and a few deer, part of the great herd of nine varieties that wanders over the rolling green expanses in this vast park of some three thousand acres.

Opposite: Woburn Abbey, 28 March 1965. The London Gate, erected in 1790, was designed by Henry Holland, a triumphal arch with the ducal arms and Ionic columns flanked by curved walls of stone which hide the gatekeepers' lodges. This grandiose entrance and south drive is rarely, if ever, used now.

Woburn Abbey, 31 March 1957. To fulfil the late eighteenth-century vogue for the oriental, the architect Henry Holland designed, in 1790, this delightful Chinese Dairy. It is sited by a fishpond and is approached by the covered arcade, which is coloured red with white for the fretted panels. Inside, the windows are of the same fretted pattern and filled with painted glass. The woodwork includes imitation bamboo trellis-work for marble-topped benches. There are wooden wall panels and painted alcoves, with arcade edges to their shelves and to the wall brackets. The purpose of the building was to display a great collection of oriental porcelain; dishes, bowls, plates, pots and jars of all sizes, shapes, patterns and colours. Originally large dishes and bowls were filled with new milk and cream, as it was used to a degree as a dairy.

Woburn, 27 January 1957. Cattle and ash trees on Horsemoor Farm looking north-east to Dolton's Farm. In the distance are firs in The Evergreens, on hills at the north end of Woburn Park.

Woburn, 27 January 1957. The farm track to the fields from Horsemoor Farm, one of the Bedford estate farms west of the village.

Woburn, 27 January 1957. Walkers on a footpath when the long shadows of trees showed the ridges and hollows in the greensand at Horsemoor Farm.

Husborne Crawley, 27 August 1966. The seventeenth-century house of Crawley Park Farm seen from the north.

Husborne Crawley, 16 October 1960. Two distinctive old houses face west to the green. One of them has been given a late Georgian front of yellow brick with pilasters and parapets.

Opposite: Husborne Crawley, 22 October 1967. An immense English elm (extreme left) towers above an orchard pasture in this view looking south towards the hilltop church. This medieval building is of local brown sandstone dug out of the greensand, but the tower is unique in the county in having blocks of different shades of green, an effect due to the mineral glauconite.

Husborne Crawley, 6 November 1965. Tall guardian English elms in their golden glory dwarf the thatched cottage facing the tiny triangular green at Church End. The cottage, during restoration and conversion to a house, was found to be late medieval with four cruck-trusses; one pair now visible in the east wall of the house at 265 Bedford Road.

Ridgmont, 3 September 1967. The Bedford estate church by Sir G.G. Scott, built in 1854-55, has a spire that is a landmark on the greensand ridge. Here, viewed from the north-west, houses in Station Road mount up the hill.

Ridgmont, 26 September 1965. The Fletton brickworks at Brogborough, from the south-west over the M1 embankment, showing its twenty-five chimneys in full production. Oxford clay was hauled up to it from Marston vale to the north. It was closed in the early 1980s.

Ridgmont, 10 September 1975. Brogborough Park was built in around 1652 on the commanding hilltop at Brogborough, by the Parliamentary Colonel and regicide John Okey (1606-62). It was a tall, square house of local brick, with a big hipped roof, stone fireplaces and central chimneystack. Locally it was known as The Round House because its rooms interconnected. It is now a gutted shell. This is the north-west front when it was the unoccupied part of a farmhouse.

Aspley Guise, 31 December 1960. The central meeting of the streets has the 1951 Festival of Britain nameboard and a shelter. The village is full of character, comprising many Victorian buildings and abundant evergreens set among the well-wooded hills of the greensand.

Aspley Guise, 19 March 1967. Aspley House was built in around 1690, but this north-west front is from around 1750 and faces the walled garden, seen here from the gate into the High Street.

Salford, 7 May 1967. A massive wych elm and English elms by the Cranfield to Salford road. These elms all died in the 1970s of Dutch elm disease. Woods on the greensand hills at Aspley Heath can be seen on the horizon.

Salford, 7 June 1958. A row of thatched cottages with dark weatherboarded walls, which stand almost opposite the church. Weatherboarding is unusual for cottages in Bedfordshire.

Cranfield, 12 September 1954. The ornate mid-Victorian Gothic schoolhouse and school, built of stone, which face the little green near the church in this hilltop village.

Cranfield, 16 August 1958. A row of charity almshouses has this elaborate stone doorway bearing the date 1885.

Eversholt, 23 March 1958. At Lower Berry End, this seventeenth-century house was demolished in the 1960s after a fire. The trees are all English elms.

Lidlington, 27 December 1965. The road west to Ridgmont (now the A507), showing roadside ashes and elms, Brussels sprouts, and rough vegetation thick with rime.

Eversholt, 21 May 1956. Eversholt is dispersed as fourteen 'Ends' in pleasant farmed country among little wooded hills of the greensand. Isolated and hedgerow trees are now few and continue to decrease. At Higher Rads End is this charming seventeenth-century cotttage, well restored.

Steppingley, 20 September 1953. The school and schoolhouse in Tudor style using local sandstone, erected in around 1870 for the Bedford estate, to a design of Henry Clutton, who had rebuilt the church in 1859-60. The school is now a private dwelling among shrubs.

Millbrook, 4 March 1961 (*above*) and 25 February 1998 (*below*). From the hilltop churchyard westward along the greensand ridge, the deep coombe is traditionally Bunyan's 'Valley of the Shadow of Death'. A thatched row of cottages has now become the village hall and additions have been made to the nearest house. The woods on the right are now part of the vast testing ground of General Motors and the view has become less distinctive and interesting.

Ampthill, 16 February 1958. Ampthill was a little country town, with several old inns at its centre. The King's Arms (originally Town) Yard is behind the former seventeenth-century inn, accessed via a coach entry, seen here when the building was a public house (it now comprises shops and apartments). The Georgian brick front, now whitened, faces the marketplace. The yard is the start of a path south to public gardens and a new, extensive housing estate.

Ampthill, 7 September 1957. A little further south in Dunstable Street are these late Georgian houses.

Ampthill, 1 May 1994. The centre, where the four original streets meet, is dominated by the early eighteenth-century 'Lanthorn' from the earlier moot hall. On the left is the 1730 front of the White Hart Hotel, a Tudor inn, and narrow Dunstable Street winds away to the south.

Ampthill, 30 September 1956. In Dunstable Street looking north to the centre of town, where the clock house faces the market place and up Church Street to the right. The clock house, by Edward Blore, was erected in 1852 for the Bedford estate.

Maulden, 12 April 1959. A pleasing cottage row that was originally built for four families but has now been made into two dwellings, which face the main road behind a garden wall of local sandstone.

Ampthill, 21 April 1961. Ampthill Park was a royal hunting ground, landscaped in 1771-72 by 'Capability' Brown for Lord Ossory. Shown here are clumps of limes and oaks which he planted, in a view that looks towards Park House and the giant brickworks (now very much smaller) at Stewartby in Marston vale. The Georgian mansion (private apartments) is now separated from its park by farmed land.

Maulden, 25 April 1954 (*above*) and 9 July 1995 (*below*). The White Hart was a quiet village pub with large horse chestnut trees shading its ground. It is now more commercialized and the garden caters for a different kind of customer.

Haynes, 17 March 1975. The tracery of large ashes is most elegant. This one is on the greensand ridge going east towards Church End. Nowadays the hedges here are more overgrown.

Clophill, 2 May 1974. Beside the motte of Cainhoe Castle, built by Norman knight Nigel d'Albini, to the north across the Flitt valley is the giant radar antenna erected by the US Air Force at Chicksands. This structure, 120ft high, was a landmark in mid-county for about thirty years.

Meppershall, 21 April 1961. In Rectory Road at the south-west end of the village are two sixteenth-seventeeth-century cottages, end-on to the road where it forks to Stondon and Shillington. They have been sympathetically restored as one dwelling; the picture above shows the north-west side. The garden, seen from Stondon Road in the picture below, has fruit trees in flower and vegetables growing.

Henlow, 1 August 1960. Henlow High Street is most attractive in the variety of its buildings of local red and yellow brick. In this south-looking view the war memorial and a white concrete telephone kiosk can be seen.

Astwick, 2 May 1974. Astwick is a tiny village on flat land by the river Ivel and next to the east boundary of the county. It has two farms, one of which, Bury Farm, is shown here. It is a seventeenth-century house surrounded by a twelfth-century moat.

Southill, 10 May 1964. Fresh leaves on elms frame this view along the road just east of Deadman's Cross, which shows numerous hedgerow trees and Keeper's Warren in the distance.

Southill, 26 September 1953. Two pairs of timber-framed, plastered and thatched estate cottages in School Lane, built in 1797 when Henry Holland was working for the estate.

Southill, 10 May 1964. An elm and two oaks in Southill Park, with more trees in the background, when people were going to visit the gardens on an open day.

Southill, 14 August 1966. The gardens of Southill Park have this classical monument to Jock, a favourite spaniel, modelled in Coade stone by George Garrard, with a verse by Samuel Whitbread (1806) and in its base a dog's drinking trough.

Old Warden, 26 March 1990. The Swiss garden is a landscape garden made 1820-25 in the contemporary fashion by Robert, third Lord Ongley of Old Warden Park. It has a tranquil pool with islets, bridges, ornaments, a Swiss cottage on a hillock, winding paths and grass among shrubs and fine trees. It was well tended by the Shuttleworth family, who added the Grotto in 1876. Bedfordshire County Council have been restoring it since 1976.

Northill, 25 November 1974. A delightful estate village, Northill's hamlet of Ickwell is centred on a green with a maypole. Here is the fourteenth-century church, mostly rebuilt in 1862, and The Crown. The one-handed church clock may be the work of the Tompion family, blacksmiths of the village, one of whom became 'the father of English watchmakers', Thomas Tompion (1639-1703).

Northill, 28 August 1974. A pair of early nineteenth-century Gothic lodges of Ickwell Bury, by the road to Cople. Now they are part of two extended dwellings.

Wrestlingworth, 12 October 1958. On the Cambridgeshire border, Wrestlingworth is now a wooded oasis in a prairie created by agribusiness. At the north end, this thatched cottage, which was once a pair, was a farmworker's home next to flat fields. It had a weedy vegetable patch and dahlias.

Wrestlingworth, 30 August 1958. In the middle of the village, a sixteenth-century timber-framed and plastered cottage end-on to the street, with a hipped end to its thatch.

Cockayne Hatley, 12 October 1958. The church, with its tall fifteenth-century tower (*above*), seen from apple orchards by Cockayne Hatley House. Now the house is called Home Farm, and all around, except for hilltop woods, is an arable prairie. In the church there is Belgian baroque carving, put there during the 1820s restoration by the Revd and Hon. Henry Cockayne Cust. The very Catholic choirstalls and backs dated 1689 (*below*) are from the Abbey of Oignies, destroyed in the Napoleonic invasion of Flanders.

Sutton, 5 April 1974. The Old Rectory is a timber-framed and plastered house from around 1550. This, its outbuildings and the church make a most pleasing group of buildings west of the ford.

Sutton, 23 September 1989. The medieval, probably late thirteenth-century, footbridge of local sandstone over the Potton Brook, looking upstream. The ford beside it is the only one on a road in the county.

Sandy, 7 August 1978. Part of The Lodge (owned by the RSPB) on Sandy Warren, a neo-Tudor house of yellow brick designed by Henry Clutton and built for Viscount Peel in 1869-77. The grounds are now a nature reserve, which includes the gardens, woods, a large pond, a disused sand quarry and a heath, which is rare for this area, where heather is being encouraged.

Potton, 9 May 1965. The north corner of Market Place in this old market town. Beyond the 1951 Festival of Britain sign is a building with hipped roof and weatherboarded side wall.

Sandy, 25 January 1986. Hazells Hall is a house from around 1660, with handsome fronts dating from 1720-40. It was restored in 1982 as apartments.

Everton, 29 August 1986. The village is on a greensand hilltop and has some market gardens. This former pair of old cottages had recently been re-thatched with reeds when this photograph was taken.

Sandy, 25 January 1986. Hazells is near Everton. The grounds of the hall were landscaped for Francis Pym by Humphry Repton in 1790-92. Many trees were planted; cedars and limes singly, oaks and sweet chestnuts in groups – trees now majestic in their maturity. Here is a typical sweet chestnut with deeply fissured trunk, bosses and burrs on boughs which are short and angular, ending with tassels of twigs. This tree is on the edge of the ridge looking towards Tempsford in the Ouse valley.

Three
The Great Ouse Valley

Willington, 25 March 1972. Sir John Gostwick rebuilt this imposing church about 1535-41, to be in keeping with his new manorial buildings. The buff stone walls are high and the windows large; he also added his chapel on the north side of the chancel, where the battlements are taller.

Willington, 15 October 1975. From the local family of Gostwick, John rose in the service of Wolsey and Henry VIII (was knighted in 1541) and, with his wealth, bought the manor of Willington in 1529. On a fresh site he built new manorial buildings of which two survive: the immense double dovecote and this two-storey dwelling, used much later as stables. Both buildings dwarf those of the present farm. This is the south end of the dwelling, a bold structure with simple details, in style around 1500, but it was probably built in the 1520s of new stone, readily available and cheaper than brick. Stepped gables were the latest fashion, and they have gargoyles at the eaves. All the windows were glazed originally with leaded lights. The stairwell was larger than for the present modern stairs. The upper floor is open to the roof timbers and its walls are plastered, The south end is shut off by a stud partition, a room with a fireplace (corbelled out externally on the east wall where the chimney has been removed) and this very finely-moulded three light window overlooking the church. The manor house was a little away to the south-west in a deer park and was described by Leland as 'A sumptuous building of brick and timber'. Thomas Cromwell stayed here briefly in September 1539 and Henry VIII on 21 October 1541.

Willington, 15 September 1975. The timbers of golden (unweathered) oak in the open roof of the two-storeyed manor house, looking to the window at the north end. The two manorial buildings are in the care of the National Trust.

Roxton, 15 August 1954. Roxton is a small village on the north bank of the Ouse. The Metcalfe family, who lived at Roxton House in the early nineteenth century, were fond of *cottage orné* with tree-trunk columns and thatch. This is their picturesque lodge by Bedford Road.

Roxton, 23 June 1995. More elaborate is the attractive Congregational church, mostly dating from 1824.

Great Barford, 6 September 1958. The south-west side of the bridge with seventeen stone arches. It was built over the river in 1429 and over the flood plain in 1704. It was widened in 1873, the red brick that was used giving it extra character. Trees now hide The Anchor (the white building) and most of the church tower.

Tempsford, 17 October 1983. Gannock House, just south of the church, is from the fifteenth century, with a pair of cross-wings, one retaining the overhang and showing impressive beams. The street here in Church End was the A1 until bypassed.

Cardington, 26 June 1988. Trinity House, the former vicarage, was built by Samuel Whitbread in 1781. The garden is opened to the public occasionally.

Cardington, 6 June 1975. Irrigation of a freshly-planted vegetable crop on a market garden by Southill Road. In the background is the embankment of the former Bedford to Hitchin railway.

Cardington, 20 April 1969. The west face of Cardington Bridge of 1778, over the Elstow Brook that drains Marston vale. The bridge was designed for Samuel Whitbread by John Smeaton, an early work before his partnership with Rennie, but it was built of brick. It is the oldest brick bridge in the county; only the cutwater caps, keystones and copings are limestone.

Harrowden, 8 November 1992. Harrowden, the hamlet in which John Bunyan was born in 1628, retains this piece of older landscape, a marshy pasture on Elstow Brook, with ancient willow pollards.

Marston Moretaine, 5 September 1965. This magnificent church had its lofty nave, aisles and porches rebuilt 1445-50. The tower stands alone to the north as at Elstow, so the nave has a large west window. The interior is spacious, with tall slender piers and wide arches.

Marston Moretaine, 4 March 1961. Marston is a Saxon 'marshy place', so its manor house had a twelfth-century moat. The present timber-framed moated house looks Tudor, with overhanging cross-wings. As Manor or Moat Farm it had great trees, many elms, and a rookery. Now it is a restaurant in a garden. During conversion, the centre was found to be fourteenth century, a hall of cruck construction with massive timbers.

Wootton, 23 February 1958. Part of a very long row of terraced eighteenth-century cottages of timber and brick which face south on the road to the church.

Bedford, 21 January 1968. St John's church with its fifteenth-century tower and the Hospital of St John (later the rectory), a twelfth-century stone building, before restoration in 1969-70 as St John House. The rector in 1653, John Gifford, converted John Bunyan to Independancy.

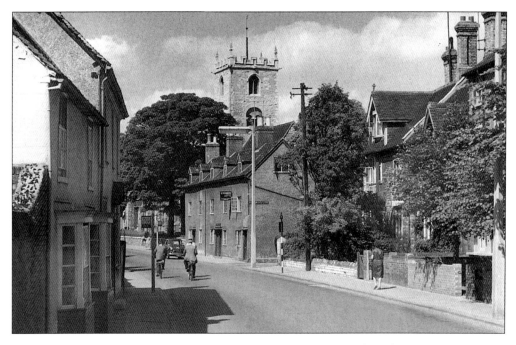

Bedford, 19 July 1959. Cardington Road, seen here looking westwards to the partly-Saxon tower of St Mary's church, had the atmosphere of a market town except for the harsh streetlamps. The row of houses (Nos 2-8 – now the Conservative Club) included the Blacksmith's Arms.

Bedford, 24 February 1978. In St John House there is fifteenth-century decoration – ostrich feathers and roses, originally red and white – on oak beams and floor joists of the timber-framed upper hall. There are also fragments of paintings on the walls.

Bedford, 19 July 1959. A little further east in Cardington Road is the elegant town house, of ashlar with a Doric porch, designed and built by the architect John Wing of Bedford for himself in 1797. It is now part of Dame Alice Harpur School.

Bedford, 14 September 1996. Bedford Museum opened in the former Higgins & Sons brewery, Castle Lane, in 1981. Varied collections put together over a century are displayed in the many well-designed galleries.

Bedford, 13 April 1969. Crofton House in St Cuthbert's Street is an early Georgian town house of red brick, with a fine classical doorcase. It was on the north-east edge of the town when it was built in around 1750.

Biddenham, 5 April 1969. Stone walls and pantiles at Church Farm, seen with elms. More recently there has been quite a lot of conversion of barns to housing here.

Biddenham, 5 April 1969. At the start of Duck End Lane stands a stone-walled house and a timber-framed and plastered row of thatched cottages. This is still a pleasing part of the original village.

Goldington, 8 May 1954. Bedford Morris Men at the finale of a dance, part of Goldington Festival, held on the green. The tall trees in the background are in the grounds of Goldington Bury, the house of which was later replaced by a tower block of flats. The village is now part of Bedford.

Bromham, 18 June 1967. The charming early nineteenth-century Gothic lodge at the south end of the drive to Bromham Hall. The original lodge was extended on the left.

Oakley, 7 February 1960. Among the trees on the right-hand side of the picture, the church is almost on its own beside the river here. The swans are on a secondary channel.

Oakley, August 1965. One of the fifteenth-century screens in the church has the only remaining rood loft in the county. Over the central opening is this original painting on the coving.

Oakley, 29 November 1982. This private residence is seen here from Stevington Road, with crows perched on riverside posts. Oakley House was made into a grand hunting lodge by Henry Holland for the fifth Duke. The Bedford estate sold it in 1920.

Oakley, 13 April 1969. In 1877 the Bedford estate owned about a tenth of the county, but had sold all outlying properties by 1914 except for Oakley, which was retained for the hunting. These estate houses dated 1865 are unusual as they are of limestone with yellow brick.

Pavenham, 24 October 1980. On the hilltop, the little fifteenth-century broach spire is a landmark. To the south, trees fill the river valley towards Stevington and an area of high ground near Turvey.

Pavenham, 20 November 1986. A footpath across The Moors by the river shows the distant village to the north-east. On the left is a row of six East Anglian elms (*Ulmus minor*), and lower on the slope are two once-pollarded ashes.

Stevington, 28 August 1965. Perhaps the loveliest limestone village in the county – even the large barns at West End Farm are built of stone, and the long barn is thatched. More recently these barns have been adapted to dwellings.

Stevington, April 1958. In the church, a quaint early sixteenth-century carving of a glutton with belly ache and feeling bilious, one of nine pew ends remounted on the Victorian pews.

Stevington, 5 April 1969. The yard of West End Farm looking south, where the height and massiveness of these stone barns can be seen. This was the start of the path leading south-west, but the route has been diverted since the conversion of the barns to housing.

Milton Ernest, 4 August 1957. The village green is a gently sloping one with the eleventh-fifteenth-century church among trees at the top. This was at a time when sensible economics prevailed: grass on the green was made into hay, no doubt a practice following on from the war years.

Milton Ernest, 29 August 1971. The substantial house and large barn of Village Farm are built of stone. The seventeenth-century house is thatched and end-on to the Felmersham road.

Bletsoe, 29 May 1960. A small village just off the main road A6(T), these timber-framed and rendered eighteenth-century cottages face north-west towards their gardens on what was once the village green.

Bletsoe, 20 January 1986. About 1½ miles north of the village, Bourne End Farm had its large house and some of its barns rebuilt in bright red brick around 1880. This handmade brick was produced only 300 yards south of the farm in 1869-98 by John William Love. He also had brickworks at Riseley and Yielden, besides working Grange Farm, Riseley.

Sharnbrook, 22 September 1968. This imposing west tower and spire dwarfs the rest of the church and is a landscape feature. The upper part of the tower, with the pretty parapet of quatrefoils and the recessed spire are from the fifteenth century. Compared with the similar spire at Harrold, the corner pinnacles and thin flying buttresses look mean, perhaps due to restoration or the use of local rather than Northamptonshire masons.

110

Felmersham, 2 August 1974. From the road to Pavenham, the village was mostly hidden by trees including many elms, but the tower of the splendid church was clear. On the far side of the valley is Sharnbrook with its church steeple.

Odell, 20 November 1982. In a rough grazing south-west of the mill, low sunlight catches the last leaves on the white willows. The pinnacled tower of the fifteenth-century church rises above the most recent Odell Castle, a 1962 square house of stone.

Harrold, 2 March 1958. The bridge here, one of the earliest of the medieval stone bridges in the county, is the most interesting one as it has developed in stages and is in three parts. This view is to the south from the middle of the six-arch river bridge. The people are on the causeway and in the passing bay; there the road curves and crosses the lower part of the flood plain on the nine-arch causeway bridge. The foot causeway, almost all medieval and comprising twenty arches, then follows the south-west side of the road. When this photograph was taken, the last of a flood was draining away from the water meadows, where the large isolated trees, including oaks, were later felled on the grounds that they were in the way of mechanical equipment to 'improve' the grazing or to cut the grass. Many more trees, mostly elms, in the distance, almost totally hid Carlton. This photograph shows clearly the long waving lines made by the outlines of the parapets.

Opposite: Odell, 2 March 1958. This view is from the east edge of the village looking south-west along the river valley, with floods receding and many isolated trees. The spires of Chellington and Harrold break the skyline (see page 9).

Harrold, 18 October 1980. A view from the foot causeway looking north to the causeway bridge and part of the river bridge. The spire, added to the church tower in around 1500, rises above the trees which hide the village.

113

Felmersham, 8 May 1960. Facing south opposite the Pavenham turning is The Sun, a stone-walled village pub. Three people are going to a wedding.

Felmersham, 29 March 1995. Thirty-five years later the building is similar, with a slated roof on the west side and steps to the garden on the right, but the surroundings are less pleasant.

Four
North Uplands

Colmworth, 12 October 1958. A vast field of Brussels sprouts at Rootham's Green, looking east to a farm at Mill End and to the cooling towers of the 1945-47 power station by the river Ouse at Little Barford. This was a very common crop in the county, but is grown less now.

Renhold, 21 January 1968. At Salph End, on the east side of the road almost opposite Abbey Farm, stand two rows of cottages, Nos 35 and 33, and nearer, Nos 31, 29 and 27, all of timber and plaster with thatch. This is how they looked when they were the homes of farm workers.

Renhold, 5 April 1990. The same rows after conversion to two detached dwellings.

Renhold, 7 June 1969. A typical pair of seventeenth-eighteenth-century timber-framed cottages in Workhouse End.

Renhold, 12 June 1983. A pool in the outer ditch of Howbury, a circular high bank (now covered with scrub) which formed a Danish camp or signal station overlooking the Ouse valley near the Danelaw boundary.

Wilden, 5 August 1957. From the roadside in Sevick End, this was a typical cottage garden belonging to the thatched yellow-brick cottage on the right. The cottage by the road had weatherboarded and pantiled outbuildings.

Ravensden, 5 October 1969. An enamelled metal advertisement of around 1912 on the yellow-brick wall of the Blacksmith's Arms facing the Kimbolton road.

Ravensden, 2 February 1969. The Case Is Altered, on Church Hill, is a country pub occupying a third of the row of six eighteenth-century Harper's Cottages. It was the parish workhouse and probably gained its name from the change of use.

Ravensden, 23 February 1995. More recently a weatherboarded barn has gone, but porches, lattice, hanging baskets, coloured lamps and a wheelie bin have appeared.

Ravensden, 12 May 1968. The lane winding over Graze Hill is part of an almost lost landscape, for it retains flowery verges, hedges and trees. At Wood End it gives this view of the buildings of Manor Farm. The house is of different periods from the fifteenth century; it is timber-framed and rendered but, in contrast, one gabled wing is weatherboarded.

Thurleigh, 22 September 1968. Approaching Church End from the west, there is sunlight on the church and Bury Farm under black cloud. The central tower of the church is from the twelfth century and the overgrown mound of the Norman castle is between the two buildings.

Thurleigh, 5 October 1969. In Church End, a good row of cottages on the hill down to The Jackal, now the only public house in the village.

Bolnhurst, 9 May 1965. The freshness and brilliance of spring is shown here by new leaves on an elm by the Kimbolton road. Ye Olde Plough was originally the fifteenth-century timber-framed and plastered farmhouse of Brayes, now rebuilt after a fire in 1989.

Keysoe, 23 June 1995. At Keysoe Row, pretty Chapel Cottage, with its rambling roses, stands between its barn and the thatched yellow-brick Baptist chapel of 1812.

Keysoe, 13 September 1958. This impressive fifteenth-century steeple, of fine ashlar with twin belfry openings, is an eye-catching feature on the open plateau, as the church stands in isolation. A miracle occurred here in 1718, when a steeplejack fell, from halfway up the spire and survived.

In Memory of the Mighty hand of
the Great God and Our Sauour —
Jesus Chrift, Who Preserued the
Life of Wil. Dickins Apr. 17. 1718 when
he was Pointing the Steepol and Fell
From the Rige of the Middel Window
in the Spiar Over the South Weft
Pinackel he Dropt Up on the Batelmen
and their Bro ack his Leg and fo ot
and Droue Down 2 Long Cope in Ston
and fo Fell to the Ground with his Nee
Upon one Standard of his Chear
When the Other End took the Groun
Which was the Neareft of Killing him
Yet when he See he was Faling Crid
Out to his Brother Lord Daniel
Wots the Matter Lord Haue Mercy
Upon me Chrift Haue Mercy Upon
me Lord Jefus Chrift Help me But
Now Almouft to the Ground
Died Nou. 29. 1759 Aged 73 Year

Keysoe, 4 December 1990. The legend stone is on the west face of the tower.

Pertenhall, 11 October 1958. A pleasing sight beyond large oaks by the road to Kimbolton is the early fifteenth-century broach spire and, in contrast, the refined classical front of red brick added in 1799 to the Old Rectory. Three generations of the King family were rectors in the eighteenth century, and they were followed in 1804 by a nephew, Thomas Martyn, who was professor of botany at Cambridge.

Keysoe, 25 March 1972. The large red-brick Baptist chapel, built in 1741 at Brook End. More recently it has become a private house, but looks the same externally.

Pertenhall, 12 October 1958. Hall Farm was a small family farm at Chadwell End, seen here with trees, and cows in a typical pasture of different grasses.

Dean, 16 June 1996. Part of the large house of former Lodge Farm, now restored and named Francis House. The plaster rendering has been stripped to expose the sixteenth-century timber frame with close studding and decoration of the smaller gables – a grand front.

Shelton, 5 August 1957. Small and lovely, this most northerly village has wide grass verges and trim hedges. Shelton Hall, now a farmhouse, is partly medieval and faces the wooded grounds of the Georgian rectory. The church is rustic and carefully conserved (by Sir Albert Richardson). Shown here are the pinnacles on the fourteenth-century west tower and gargoyles on the angles of the south aisle. Inside are late Norman capitals.

Melchbourne, 18 July 1974. Five of the row of eight early eighteenth-century estate cottages which line The Street and face Melchbourne Park. Fire destroyed the second row in 1961.

Souldrop, 2 August 1974. North of the village, the Forty Foot Lane is the parish boundary, a cross-country drover's road named for its width between the bordering hedges. It may follow a prehistoric route to the south-west. Here a narrow drive leads to Blackmere Farm. A mass of yellow hawkweed blooms on the wide verge.

Riseley, 29 May 1960. In Gold Street, looking uphill, there is space between the dwellings, a timber-framed and plastered cottage beyond its privy and barn, a Victorian cottage of chequered red and yellow brick behind the sycamore, and a row of three cottages with rendered walls. Vegetables are being grown.

Wymington, 14 October 1961. In the hills above the Nene valley, the glory of this village is its church, rebuilt 1350-90 by local and Northamptonshire masons for John Curteys, a wealthy wool merchant. The interior is crowded with ornate detail, many arches, faint colours of paintings, and the founder's tomb with 1391 brass under an ogee arch. Shown here is the two-storeyed porch, vaulted inside, also rich ornamentation on the tower and crowning spire, the last part to be finished.